50/50
Chance of An Unspoken Life!

Written by:

Rochelle Baxter

To order additional copies of this book, contact:
Xlibris
844-714-8691
www.Xlibris.com
Orders@Xlibris.com

ISBN: Softcover   978-1-6641-2878-1
         EBook   978-1-6641-2877-4

Print information available on the last page

Rev. date: 10/06/2020

Dedication

Mom Cherry, Sister April and Brother Aaron Baxter. True love for Brother Julian Baxter. True love for Grandmother Loretta Stewart, Grandfather William Stewart and Uncle Bill Stewart. Shout out to: Aunt Barbara Rhodus, Cousins: Ondelaia, Camya, Eagel, Danithia, and Carol Roach.

Much love to: Cousins, Vonnie, Rodney, Dana, Lydia, Emery, Adrienne, Kellie, Jonathan, Aunt Sandra, Cee-cee, Cynthia, Tanya, Keisha, Leon, Carl, Ronald, Aunt Lillie May and Rashawn. My three nephews Asire, Amir and Caree.

Additional Greetings to: Keisha and Ms. Daisy. I can't forget about Cousins: Dondre, Marissa, Malea, Maicen, Mansa, Carl Jr and Cristian. Members of the Baxter Family: Grandmother Addie Mitchell, Father Larry Baxter, Aunt Lauren Baxter, Aunt Hattie Patterson, Aunt Lita Moses, Aunt Linda Moore, Cousins: Willie Johnson and Karen Johnson, also cousin Colin, cousin Wendy Moore and many others in the Baxter Family.

Much Love to: cousin Mary Lou, cousin Bubba, Aunt Joe, Aunt Essie, and cousin Makea. Love to: Brother G and Sharon Gardner, Pearsall Family and Cruickshank Family. Additional Good Friends: Paul and Cynthia Harris, Lambert and Sarah Brown, James and Mary Rogers, Mark and Jennifer Stanford.

Table of Contents

50/50
Chance of An
Unspoken Life!

My Big, Funny Family!

New!

Lovely!

Different!

Intelligent!

Cool!

Caring!

Welcoming!

Encouraging!

Enormous!

Lively!

Angelic!

Vibrant!

Generous!

Beautiful!

Warm!

Cozy!

Creative!

Passionate!

Amusing!

Awesome!

Graceful!

Poppin!

Sign,

I love my Big Family!
Family, Faithfulness, Friends!

A Diligent Person!

A diligent person is caring, supportive,
submissive, wise, smart and romantic.
Hardworking, sharing his or her heart to everyone.

Thoughtful, loyal, forgiving.
A caretaker, spiritually strong.
Thifty, hopeful, a cheerful person.

Everyone should hope and pray
that they are a diligent person
today and forever!

Your true rock forever!

Life in the City!

Life can be difficult.

Life can be kind.

Life can be harsh.

Life can be wild.

Life can be elegant.

Life can be fulfilling.

Life can be overwhelming.

Life can be busy.

So far, we have to make the best

out of life!

Life can be fun, but challenging!

My Mother, My Sister!

Mind, Body, Soul!

My Mother, My Sister!

Heart, Rock, Solid!

Angel, Innocent, Brave!

Friend, Good Friend, Best Friend!

Love, Passion, Togetherness!

Beauty, Wise, Brilliant!

Family, Relative, Kin!

My Mother, My Sister!

Love Forever!

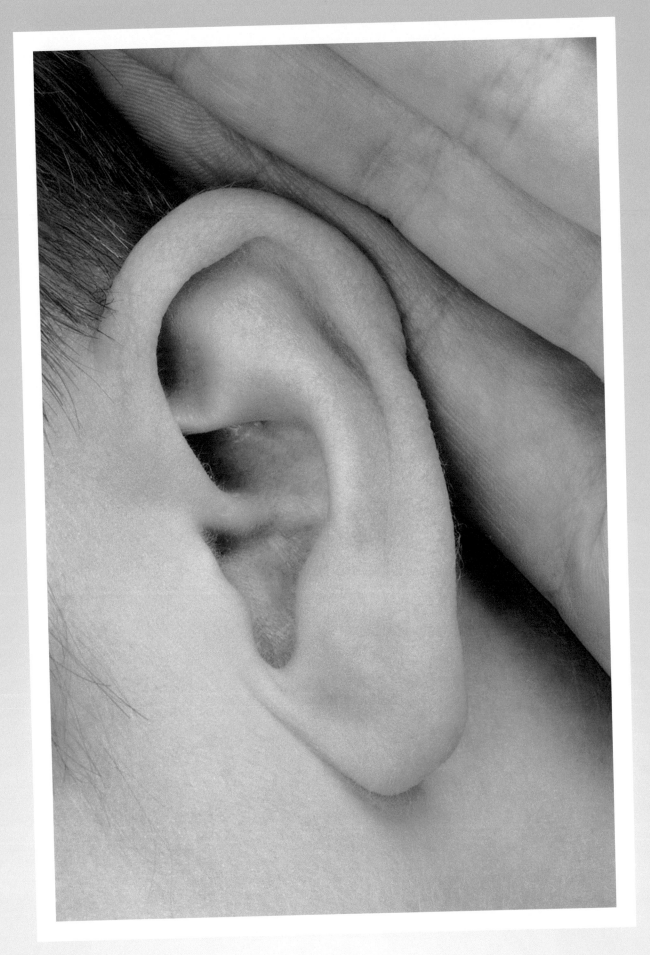

Gossip Girl!

I will tell you everything from A to Z
      because I'm a Gossip Girl.
I will tell you everything that happened
      at work and at home.
I will tell you everything that occurred
      around my way and my neighborhood.
I will tell you who said what and
      how it was said.
I will tell you what the news reporter
      and radio commentator mentioned.
I will smile and grin with you,
      but I will tell you the facts of life.
I will tell you the bitter with
      the sweet.
I will always tell you the truth,
      and I will never lie.
Last, but not least, I don't care
      if you don't like me
because I'm a Gossip Girl.

Written by Gossip Girl!

My Brother's!

Boys and Gentlemen!

Brother A! and Brother J!

My Brother's!

Men I can talk too!

Handsome and good-looking!

My Friend's forever!

I Love you!

I think about you everyday!

My precious stones!

Always in my heart!

My Brother's!

Deep and Lasting Love!

Aunts!

Aunt! Auntie B!
Hi Ladies!
How's Pop doing?
Let me speak to Shelly Belly!
Black Chinese slippers!
Oh!
Lord, Jesus!
Let me get up from here!
What's going on?
Bubba called me!
Look here!
White Castle on half-days!
Aunt B
Auntie L
Words of Wisdom!
You told me what "Family means!"

F	-	Faith
A	-	Authentic
M	-	Meaning
I	-	Insight
L	-	Love
Y	-	Yielding

Love always,
Aunties

Grandparents of Grace!

My grandmother, Mrs. S, meant the world to me.
Her brown eyes were filled with light.
Her smile was catchy.
Her beautiful spirit was always cheerful.
She loved everyone to the end.
She would always be loved and missed.
My grandfather, Mr. S, although I never met you,
I look forward to seeing you in the New World.

My grandmother, Mother M, was a woman of "Rocky Roads."
She loved to wear hats.
She spoke her mind.
She was a woman of success.
She will be missed from communicating by telephone.
She would always be loved and missed.
Grandparents Are The Best!

Cousins!

Cousins are like brothers and sisters.

They are travelling partners.

They share your friends and clothes.

They spend lots of time at your home.

They call you on the telephone.

They sing and play games with you.

They bake chocolate chip cookies.

They share with you.

They laugh with you.

They comb and brush your hair.

Cousins are truly like brothers and sisters.

Your Cousins Forever!

Uncle!

Uncle B, an uncle you could never forget.

He was loving and caring.

He would come around his family to help,

when we would least expect him.

He would take his nieces and nephews to school.

He would take us to the playground to play.

He took us to the Doctor when we were sick.

Uncle B told jokes.

He liked to eat peanut butter and jelly sandwiches

with sliced bananas.

Uncle B would never be forgotten.

Uncle, You Are Remembered!

People!

Black or White!

Brave and Afraid!

Good or Bad!

Free or Confined!

Rich or Poor!

Innocent or Guilty!

Tall or short!

Sweet or Bitter!

Hot or Cold!

Sober or Drunk!

A person can take on different forms throughout his/her life!

Blessings!

I thought, I had the real thing,
Until I met you!
I thought I was living comfortably,
Until you brought me a home!
I thought I was wearing jewelry,
Until you gave me diamonds!
I thought I was travelling,
Until you showed me the world!
I thought I had it all,
Until I found you!
I thought I was blessed,
Until you really, really blessed me!

True Friends!

A man or a woman who would not lie.

A person who is honest.

A human-being who listens.

A child who hugs.

A mother who kisses on the cheek.

A father who holds their child by the hand.

A wife who looks and stares at her lover.

A husband who touches and rubs his true heart.

A grandmother who smiles.

A grandfather who blesses others.

True Friends Rock!

Family, Faithfulness, Friends!

Family Gatherings!

Lots of cooking and food!

Much laughter and smiles!

Many pictures and videotaping!

Memories old and new!

Dancing to the guitar and drums!

Unending hugs and kisses!

Welcoming In-Laws and Newborns!

Playing card games and video games!

Speeches about life and the world around us!

Listening to Jazz and Salsa music!

At the Park In the 80's!

In the park with Grandma,
      Playing by the Benches.
In the park with Grandma,
      On the swings.
In the park with Grandma,
      Going to the circus.
In the park with Grandma,
      Only in the Summertime.
In the park with Grandma,
      Building a Sandcastle.
In the park with Grandma,
      Eating Bologna Sandwiches.
In the park with Grandma,
      Preaching Good News.
In the park with Grandma,
      Running after Pigeons.
In the park with Grandma,
      Drinking the Fountain Water.
In the park with Grandma,
      Jumping rope.

At the Beach In 1988!

Riding on the bus.

Carrying a Cooler.

Wearing shorts and sneakers.

Preparing food on the grill.

Putting my feet in the sand.

Playing Hide - N – Seek.

Drinking water and lemonade.

Throwing the Frisbee in the air.

Enjoying my Yo-Yo.

Feeling the cool breeze.

Having Fun in 1990!

Taking the "D" train.

It is Easter Sunday.

I put on clothes.

Walking to purchase Vanilla Ice Cream.

I can't wait to drive the "Bumper Cars".

I love the ride called the "whip".

I was hurrying to board the "Ferris Wheel".

By the way, to use the bathroom was 25 cents.

I enjoyed eating hotdogs and french fries.

Cereza! (Queen B)

Cereza is sweet fruit during all her motherdays.

She is the greatest.

She is a hard-working person.

She took care of her children.

She is well-educated.

She is beautiful in person and in spirit.

She is a Queen.

She can dress like a model.

She speaks with class and elegance.

She is brilliant in American sign Language.

Cereza is sweet fruit during all her motherdays.

Sister Nippie!

Sister Nippie is Sister love.

She is a wonderful helper.

She is an excellent teacher.

She is slim.

She is a great cook.

She likes to read in the night time.

She is one of the best in Math.

She likes to work with children.

She likes to play Pac-Man.

She likes to huddle on the couch.

She has beautiful feet.

Sister Nippie is Sister love.

Brother AB!

Brother AB is a part of my brotherhood.

He is kind.

He is smart.

He is an excellent writer.

He is good in speed Reading.

He is gentle.

He is "The Man."

He is great at Basketball.

He is tall.

He is an extraordinary Dancer.

He is cool.

Brother AB is a part of my brotherhood.

Brother J!

A family man!

Oh boy, how you have matured!

Sounds wise!

Oh boy, how you have matured!

Working and surviving!

Oh boy, how you have matured!

Three children, maybe a fourth on the way!

Oh boy, how you have matured!

Rapping and Producing Music!

Oh boy, how you have matured!

Wondering about the Future, but serious about life!

Oh boy, how you have matured!

A positive role-model for your sons!

Oh boy, how you have matured!

Happiness!

Heavy burdens, carry!

Happiness will come, if not today, Tomorrow!

Broken Souls, torn hearts, always hurting badly!

Happiness will come, if not today, Tomorrow!

Sad, Angry; feeling crabby!

Happiness will come, if not today, Tomorrow!

Waiting and waiting and waiting for "Daddy" to bring candy!

Happiness will come, if not today, Tomorrow!

Feeling the "Blues" so I speak sassy!

Happiness will come, if not today, Tomorrow!

Hair uncombed, dressing sloppy!

Happiness will come, if not today, Tomorrow!

I told you "I Don't Care" You are really nasty.

Happiness will come, if not today, Tomorrow!

Now, I am feeling fancy!

Happiness will come, if not today, Tomorrow!

Singing, Dancing, Laughing, Oh the beat is so catchy!

Happiness will come, if not today, Tomorrow!

Hats, scarfs, suits, new shoes, education, life, what;

I am classy!

Happiness will come, if not today, Tomorrow!

Love!

Beauty, warmth, and gentleness;

   Truly God's gift from above.

It is never rough.

It captivates the inner soul, and hatred is removed.

Soft, smooth, silky, and filled with red puff.

No push, No fight, No shove!

With love, there is always room to improve!

Lightness, Brightness, and Whiteness like a dove.

Holding hands, tightly as a glove.

Everyday, walking with the spirit of love!

Faithfulness!

Many different scenarios, many different cases.

Trying to stay safe.

Praying for the "Human Race".

Running, jumping, and hopping to keep up the pace.

Thankful for family and friends, bowing down to give grace.

Imperfect for sure, but "Golden Paths" that lead to faithful traces.

Life has not been easy, but we can put on "Shiny Faces".

From above comes many, many praises.

We are, definitely, clothed with faithful laces.

Let someone in your personal space!

Faith, Strength, and Endurance; Our hands we will raise!

Family, Faithfulness, Friends!

Our Human Nature!

Everyone must try to connect!

High expectations expect!

Someone is feeling bad, please detect!

Work habits and attitudes, always perfect!

One another, cherish and protect!

Unkind words and speech, reject!

You don't always have to be correct!

But excellent word choices, select!

Respect is such a wonderful subject!

Never leave it unchecked!

Respect! Respect! Respect!

Let us practice, practice every aspect!

Kind is the New Cool!

Being kind is never blind!

Look around, and you will find!

Smile, your teeth, never grind!

Walk a fine line!

With kindness, honesty, and humility, rise and shine!

Think before you speak and use your mind!

Put kindness in your heart, and forever bind!

Being mean and cruel, leave behind!

Kindness has a new look and design!

Kind is the New Cool, and it has been defined!

Displaying Goodness!

What is Goodness?

Is it Rudeness?

Is it Madness?

Is it Sadness?

Is it Sweetness?

Is it Greatness?

Is it Completeness?

Hoping Goodness is displaying shrewdness with kindness!

Never displaying, Goodness with Badness!

Always remember, display Goodness with

plenty of Gladness!!!!

Love, Love, Love!

Often, Love should be spoken!

However, it makes many frozen!

Sad, but hearts have been broken!

Now, we should change our slogan!

Love, Love, Love!

It is a small token!

Nonetheless, let's start by changing our emotions!

Listen and pray before we think about having another explosion!

Can we meditate and express how Love can embody Our Devotion?

Next time, when we have said or done something wrong,

can we try to change that notion?

Love, Love, Love!

A New Kind of Spin!

Say "Thank You" and "Please;" it is never a sin.
Pack a few clothes and place it in a bin.
Add pieces of candy and drop it in a tin.
You never know who may need clothes, a gift,
a small treat from a friend, or perhaps a kin.
If you show mildness, you will definitely win.
It's nice to know, if you never listen to what I
say, you will still be my friend.

Death!

Unspoken words, so painful!

Guilt and sadness, feeling so shameful!

Many loved ones gone; angry thoughts so hateful.

Pray, Pray, Pray now and again because many precious
moments to be grateful.

Dead family and friends were faithful.

Moving forward, words and thoughts would be tasteful.

Once in a while, physical, mental, and emotional trauma
so hurtful!

Thinking about the good times and good memories were so gainful.

Helps the pain and stops us from being so playful.

Many days, wishing for words of wisdom and faith.

Because our "Loved Ones" sayings were never wasteful.

Printed in the United States
By Bookmasters